TOP 10 MEN'S TENNIS PLAYERS

Andre Christopher

SPORTS TOP 10

Enslow Publishers, Inc.

44 Fadem Road   PO Box 38
Box 699   Aldershot
Springfield, NJ 07081   Hants GU12 6BP
USA   UK

Library of Congress Cataloging-in-Publication Data

Christopher, Andre.
     Top 10 men's tennis players / Andre Christopher.
        p. cm. — (Sports top 10)
     Includes bibliographical references and index.
     Summary: Profiles the lives and careers of tennis players Andre Agassi,
Arthur Ashe, Bjorn Borg, Don Budge, Jimmy Connors, Pancho Gonzales, Rod
Laver, John McEnroe, Pete Sampras, and Bill Tilden.
     ISBN 0-7660-1009-0
     1. Tennis players—Biography—Juvenile literature. [1. Tennis players.]
I. Title. II. Series.
GV994.A1C46   1998
796.342'092'2
[B]—DC21   97-19979
                                                CIP
                                                AC

Printed in the United States of America

10 9 8 7 6 5 4 3 2 1

CONTENTS

INTRODUCTION

WHO ARE THE GREATEST MEN'S TENNIS PLAYERS of all time? Fans often have a tough time trying to identify the greats because of the many changes tennis has gone through.

In the 1920s and 1930s, when Big Bill Tilden and Don Budge became legends, men's tennis was a different game from the professional tennis played today. It was a game played by "gentlemen." Players wore long white pants and used heavy racquets made of solid wood. Matches were played on grass courts. The great tournaments, Wimbledon, the U.S. Championships, the Australian Championships, and the French Championships, were for amateurs only. Professional tennis players could not participate.

Today's stars such as Pete Sampras and Andre Agassi play with much lighter racquets made of composite materials. They wear baggy shorts and leave their shirts untucked. The Grand Slam tournaments are open to both professional and amateur tennis players. Grass courts have nearly disappeared. In 1996, only six of eighty-four tournaments were played on grass. With these different conditions, it is difficult to compare a player from one era to a player from another.

We based our list on several factors. Each player has won at least one of the four Grand Slam tournaments, the most important tournaments in the world. Some had explosive serves; others wowed fans with their sheer athleticism and endurance. All must have been able to anticipate their opponents and react quickly.

There are some noticeable absences in this book. Players such as Lew Hoad, Ken Rosewall, and Ivan Lendl were amazing players. They dominated the game in their prime. The influence of the ten men we have included, however, goes beyond the tennis court. Each has played an important part in the historical development of tennis.

Pancho Gonzales became a major champion in the late 1940s, and he won the U.S. pro championship a record seven straight years. As a Mexican American, Gonzales showed that a person did not have to be white or rich to be a great tennis player. He opened the door for all to excel in tennis.

Rod Laver won the Grand Slam twice, in 1962 and in 1969. No one else has won two Grand Slams. That is why most experts consider Laver to be the greatest men's tennis player of all time.

GRAND SLAM SINGLES CHAMPIONSHIPS

PLAYER	AUST.	FRENCH	WIMB.	U.S.	YRS. #1
ANDRE AGASSI	1995		1992	1994	1994
ARTHUR ASHE	1970		1975	1968	
BJORN BORG		1974, 1975 1978, 1979 1980, 1981	1976, 1977 1978, 1979 1980		1979–80
DON BUDGE	1938	1938	1937, 1938	1937, 1938	1937–38
JIMMY CONNORS	1974		1974, 1982	1974, 1976 1978, 1982 1983	1974–78
PANCHO GONZALEZ				1947, 1948	1949
ROD LAVER	1960, 1962 1969	1962, 1969	1961, 1962, 1968, 1969	1962, 1969	1961–62 1968–69
JOHN MCENROE			1981, 1983 1984	1979, 1980 1981, 1984	1981–84
PETE SAMPRAS	1994, 1997		1993, 1994 1995, 1997	1990, 1993 1995, 1996	1993–97
BILL TILDEN			1920, 1921 1930	1920, 1921 1922, 1923 1924, 1925 1929	1920–25

AUST.=Australian Championships*   **U.S.**=U.S. Championships*
FRENCH=French Championships*   **YRS. #1**=Years ranked at #1
WIMB.=Wimbledon

*Since 1968 the tournaments in Australia, France, and the U.S. have been referred to as the Australian Open, French Open, and the U.S. Open.

ANDRE AGASSI

Concentrating on his opponent, Agassi gets ready to return the serve. Agassi excels at international competition. He won the gold medal at the 1996 Summer Olympics.

ANDRE AGASSI

PEOPLE CALLED ANDRE AGASSI a lot of things during his first eight years as a tennis pro. They called him a show-off. They called him a phony. They called him a waste because he had the talent to be one of the all-time great players, but he didn't try hard enough.

No one ever called him a champion, however, until after the 1994 U.S. Open.

Agassi charged through the 1994 tournament playing the best tennis of his life. He beat five players ranked higher than he was, something no one had done in forty years. After he defeated Michael Stich in the singles final, Agassi dropped to his knees and shouted, "I don't believe it! I don't believe it!"

Agassi had finally proved himself to be a real champion. He was on his way to being No. 1.

"Well, I was No. 1 these two weeks," Agassi said. "So if I can do it for these two weeks, I can somehow now take another step and make it more often."[1]

Soon after defeating Pete Sampras to win the 1995 Australian Open, a Grand Slam tournament like the U.S. Open, Agassi achieved his lifelong dream of being ranked No. 1.

Before Agassi could even walk as a little boy, his father, Mike Agassi, had put a tennis racquet in his hand. By the time Andre was six years old, he was hitting with tennis legends such as Bjorn Borg, Ilie Nastase, and Bobby Riggs on the tennis courts at the Las Vegas hotel where his father worked.

"Andre had the desire," Mike Agassi said. "I don't know if the desire was just to please his parents, but he had it."[2]

When Andre was thirteen, his father sent him to Florida to learn tennis from Nick Bollettieri, a famous tennis coach. By the time he was sixteen, Andre turned pro. He became one of the most famous tennis players in the world.

Andre Agassi was ranked No. 3 in the world when he was eighteen years old. A few years later, he won Wimbledon, the most famous tournament in tennis.

But Agassi had bad habits that prevented him from becoming the best player he could be. He ate a lot of junk food, and he didn't practice hard.

Agassi's ranking dropped. He injured his wrist so badly he had to have surgery. After his wrist surgery in December 1993, no one was sure he would be as good as he had been.

But Agassi came back even better, thanks to the help of his new coach, Brad Gilbert, a former top 10 pro. Gilbert convinced Agassi to train hard and eat right. The 1994 U.S. Open was among twelve tournaments Agassi won during 1994 and 1995.

Although he struggled to keep playing that well for most of 1996, Agassi was able to prove he was still a great player by winning the gold medal at the Olympics. "To win a Grand Slam in the sport of tennis is the biggest thing you can accomplish inside your sport," he said. "But the Olympics is the biggest thing you can do in sports. To win a gold medal is what it's all about. This is the greatest accomplishment I've ever had in this sport."[3]

ANDRE AGASSI

BORN: April 29, 1970, Las Vegas, Nevada.

PLAYS: Right-handed, two-handed backhand.

YEAR TURNED PRO: 1986.

GRAND SLAM TOURNAMENT SINGLES TITLES: (3); Australian Open (1995), U. S. Open (1994), Wimbledon (1992).

HONORS: U.S. Davis Cup team, 1988–93, 1995, 1997; top 5 in all-time U.S. Davis Cup singles victories (24), 1996 Olympic Gold Medal.

Hustling across the court, Andre Agassi gets into position to make another forehand smash. Agassi's style and talent have made him a fan favorite.

ARTHUR ASHE

ALMOST IN ONE MOTION, Arthur Ashe made sports history. He tossed the tennis ball high and blasted his serve to Tom Okker's backhand. Okker chipped the ball back to Ashe. Running to the net as he always did after one of his booming first serves, Ashe hit a backhand volley from just inside the service line. Okker, one of the fastest players in the game, ran as fast as he could to get to the ball, but he never touched it.

Arthur Robert Ashe Jr. had won the 1968 U.S. Open Tennis Championships.

It was the first time the U.S. National Championships had been "open" to both amateur and professional players. Ashe, an amateur, was the first American man in thirteen years to win the tournament. He was the first African-American man to win *any* of the Grand Slam tournaments.

"This week, at least, Ashe proved himself the best player in the world," the legendary Jack Kramer said on TV.[1]

Ashe started playing tennis when he was six years old. A man named Ronald Charity taught him how to play on the courts near the Ashe house in Richmond, Virginia.

Soon, Ashe was so good, Charity told Dr. Robert Walter Johnson about him. Dr. Johnson taught tennis to many of the top African-American players. Ashe spent summers with Dr. Johnson from the time he was ten years old until he was eighteen. He became the best African-American player in the country.

Some tournaments would not allow Ashe to play because he was African American. But he did not get

ARTHUR ASHE

Arthur Ashe looks to blast the ball past his opponent. In 1968 Ashe became the first African-American man to win a Grand Slam tournament.

discouraged. Ashe was on his way to becoming the best player in the world.

Ashe won fifty championships (singles or doubles) after the 1968 U.S. Open, including Wimbledon in 1975. He defeated Jimmy Connors in one of the biggest upsets in tournament history. But Ashe was not surprised.

"I believed that I would win," he said. "I don't mean I thought I would win. I *understood* that I would win."[2]

Then, suddenly, in 1979, Ashe had a heart attack and had to stop playing tennis. He stayed involved in tennis as captain of the U.S. Davis Cup team from 1981 through 1985. The U.S. team won two Davis Cup titles while Ashe was captain.

After Davis Cup, Ashe began the most important phase of his life. He became active in trying to make the world a fair place for all people, especially for young boys and girls. He also wrote a series of books, *A Hard Road to Glory*, about the history of African-American athletes.

The books had just been published in 1988 when Ashe learned that he had AIDS, a very serious disease. He got the disease from infected blood he received during a 1983 heart operation. But he kept working to make the world a better place, as he had always done. In fact, Ashe didn't tell most people he had AIDS until 1992.

After everyone knew, Ashe established a foundation to help find a cure for AIDS. The world's top men's and women's tennis players helped to raise money for the foundation by playing matches for fun the day before the 1992 U.S. Open.

Five months later, Ashe died because of AIDS.

"He fought hard," said his wife, Jeanne Moutoussamy-Ashe, "and as in his tennis days, it was always how he played the game."[3]

ARTHUR ASHE

BORN: July 10, 1943, Richmond, Virginia.

DIED: February 6, 1993.

COLLEGE: UCLA.

PLAYED: Right-handed, one-handed backhand.

YEAR TURNED PRO: 1969.

GRAND SLAM TOURNAMENT SINGLES TITLES: (3); Australian Open (1970), U.S. Open (1968); Wimbledon (1975).

GRAND SLAM TOURNAMENT DOUBLES TITLES: (2); French Open (1971), Australian Open (1977).

HONORS: *Sports Illustrated* Sportsman of the Year, 1992; enshrined in International Tennis Hall of Fame, 1985; U.S. Davis Cup captain, 1981–85; U.S. Davis Cup team, 1963, 1965–70, 75, 1977–78; top 5 in all-time U.S. Davis Cup singles victories (27); president, Association of Tennis Professionals (ATP), 1974–75.

Arthur Ashe pounces down with cat-like quickness to return a low volley. Aside from being a spectacular athlete, Ashe was also an accomplished writer.

BJORN BORG

Bjorn Borg's grass court ability is possibly unmatched. At one point he won five consecutive Wimbledon titles, the most important of all the tournaments played on grass.

As JOHN MCENROE PREPARED TO SERVE, he glanced across the net at Bjorn Borg, almost in wonder. Borg had already lost seven match points to McEnroe—five in the fourth set tiebreaker—but he would not give in. "Losing that tiebreaker would have broken the spirit of most players," McEnroe said later.[1]

Borg was not most players. Not only was he the coolest, most unemotional player, but by that summer day in 1980, Borg had already won five French Open singles titles, more than any man in the tournament's modern era. If he could win this match, he would win his fifth consecutive Wimbledon singles title, something no man in the modern era of tennis had ever done.

McEnroe served the ball to Borg's backhand and rushed to the net. Borg smacked the ball toward the middle of the court. McEnroe hit a weak forehand volley and then watched as Borg ripped a backhand winner past him. Game. Set. Match.

Borg dropped to his knees and leaned back, looking toward the sky. He had made tennis history.

"I never knew how good he was going to be, but the possibility was there early for him to be the best ever," said Lennart Bergelin, Borg's coach.[2]

Borg did not plan to be a great tennis player when he was a boy growing up in Sodertalje, Sweden. "My first love was ice hockey," he said.[3] But his father gave him a tennis racquet when he was nine years old, and two years later, Borg won his first tennis tournament. He dropped hockey and began playing tennis all the time, from morning to night.

In 1972, when Borg was fifteen, he was selected to play for Sweden in the Davis Cup. He defeated Onny Parun of New Zealand to become the youngest player to win a Davis Cup match.

Two years later, Borg won the Italian Open and the French Open, the most important clay court tournaments in the world. Two years after that, in 1976, he won his first Wimbledon. Borg was on his way to greatness.

Borg won so often in the 1970s that Ilie Nastase, the man he defeated for the 1976 Wimbledon singles title, said, "They should send Borg away to another planet. We play tennis. He plays something else."[4]

Borg is the only man to win the French Open and Wimbledon in the same year for three years in a row. He is the only man to have won at least one Grand Slam tournament for eight years in a row (1974–81) during the open era.

The only tournament Borg could never win during his eleven years in pro tennis was the U.S. Open. He played in the tournament ten times, and his best finish was runner-up—four times.

"That is the one I think of," Borg said, "but it is not a regret."[5]

The greatest days of Borg's career ended after he lost the 1981 U.S. Open final to McEnroe. He announced his retirement in 1983, tried a comeback in 1991, and began playing on the senior tennis tour in 1993. But Borg had already left his mark on the sport.

BJORN BORG

BORN: June 6, 1956, Sodertalje, Sweden.

PLAYS: Right-handed, two-handed backhand.

YEAR TURNED PRO: 1973.

GRAND SLAM TOURNAMENT SINGLES TITLES: (11); French Open
(1974–75, 1978–81), Wimbledon (1976–80).

HONORS: Enshrined in International Tennis Hall of Fame, 1987;
Swedish Davis Cup team, 1972–75, 1978–80.

Bending for the ball, Bjorn Borg rips a backhand. Borg was
inducted into the International Tennis Hall of Fame in 1987 and
then returned to competitive tennis in 1991.

DON BUDGE

NO ONE HAD EVER WON the championships of Australia, France, Great Britain, and the United States in the same year. Doing so is called winning the Grand Slam. In 1938, Budge needed to win only the U.S. National Championship and he would become the first person to win the Grand Slam.

But Budge had to beat Gene Mako to win the U.S. title. Mako was Budge's good friend and doubles partner. "Gene was playing the best singles of his life," Budge said.[1]

At that time, however, no one was playing better than Budge. He was ranked No. 1 in 1937 and 1938. He defeated Mako 6-3, 6-8, 6-2, 6-1.

Budge had won the Grand Slam of tennis. He set the standard for greatness in his sport.

"I take a certain whimsical pride in not only having won the Grand Slam," Budge said, "but in a sense, having created it as well."[2]

As a boy, Budge did not really like tennis. He did not play any tennis at all from the time he was eleven years old until he was fifteen.

Then one day in June 1930, Budge's brother Lloyd joked with Don that he should play in the California state boys' championship. Don did. He won the tournament. Within three years, Don Budge became the United States Tennis Association national junior champion.

When Budge was chosen for the U.S. Davis Cup team in 1935, he knew then that he wanted to be a really great player.

"I thought, 'Gee, maybe I can be the best player in the

DON BUDGE

In 1938, Don Budge defeated Gene Mako to win the U.S. National Championship, becoming the first person to ever win the Grand Slam.

world—at least I am knocking on the door now,'" Budge said.[3]

Fred Perry, from Great Britain, was the No. 1 player in the world in 1935 and 1936. In 1936, Budge was the second-best amateur player in the world. Then when Perry turned pro at the end of 1936, that left Budge as the best.

Hardly anyone could beat Budge in 1937 and 1938. Before he won the Grand Slam in 1938, he played a match in 1937 that people call the greatest in the history of tennis.

The match was almost like winner-take-all for the Davis Cup. Budge was playing Germany's Baron Gottfried von Cramm. The match was so important that Adolf Hitler called von Cramm before the players went on court.

Von Cramm won the first two sets. Budge won the next two. Von Cramm went ahead 4-1 in the fifth and final set. It looked like he would win.

As the players changed sides of the court, Budge told his captain, "Don't worry, Cap. I won't let you down. I'll win this one if it kills me."[4]

Budge came back to win seven of the next nine games. He won the match as he ran hard to hit a forehand and then dived to the ground to stop himself. The crowd roared! Budge had won!

The United States later won the Davis Cup for the first time since 1926.

"No man, living or dead, could have beaten either man that day," said U.S. Davis Cup captain Walter Pate.

But Budge beat von Cramm. Budge was the best in the world.

Don Budge

BORN: June 13, 1915, Oakland, California.

COLLEGE: University of California at Berkeley.

PLAYS: Right-handed, one-handed backhand.

YEAR TURNED PRO: 1938.

GRAND SLAM TOURNAMENT SINGLES TITLES: (6); Australian Championships (1938), French Championships (1938), U.S. Championships (1937–38), Wimbledon (1937–38).

GRAND SLAM TOURNAMENT DOUBLES TITLES: (4); Wimbledon (1937–38); U.S. Championships (1936, 1938).

HONORS: Enshrined in International Tennis Hall of Fame, 1964; Associated Press Athlete of the Year, 1937, 1938; Sullivan Award, 1937; U.S. Davis Cup team, 1935–38.

Don Budge led the United States team to a Davis Cup victory in 1937. It was their first win in eleven years. On the left is former tennis pro Fred Perry.

"PLAYING [JIMMY] CONNORS IS LIKE FIGHTING Joe Frazier," Dick Stockton said. "The guy's always coming at you. He never lets up."[1]

If no one believed Stockton when he said those words after losing to Connors in the semifinals of Wimbledon in 1974, Connors himself provided proof two months later. After beating Ken Rosewall to win Wimbledon, Connors crushed Rosewall 6-1, 6-0, 6-1 to win the U.S. Open.

It was the most lopsided men's championship match in U.S. Open history. After the match, some people suggested that Connors should have let up a little bit. He was twenty-two years old. Rosewall was thirty-nine, practically an old man as far as athletes go.

But Connors didn't care. He played tennis as if his life depended on it.

"My mom," Connors said, "led me by the hand and said, 'We're going to the tennis courts. If you want to play, play hard.'"[2]

Connors's mother, Gloria, and his grandmother, Bertha, taught him to play tennis on a court they built behind their house in Belleville, Illinois. Connors was about three years old when they started. For most of his life, Connors's mom was really his only coach. She taught him the game very well.

Connors turned pro in 1972, the year after he won the National Collegiate Athletic Association (NCAA) championship in his first year at the University of California at Los Angeles (UCLA). He wasn't really liked by other pro players, however. He wouldn't play in the Davis Cup. He

Jimmy Connors displays his championship form. Connors turned pro in 1972 after winning the NCAA championship while at UCLA.

JIMMY CONNORS

wouldn't join the players' association. On the court, he often behaved very badly.

"I was an animal early in my career," Connors said.[3]

But Connors helped to make tennis more popular than it had ever been. No matter how bad his behavior was, everyone knew he was a great player. He always tried to win every point in every match.

The U.S. Open title Connors won in 1974 was one of fifteen championships he won that year. That was the most anyone had ever won in one year. Connors won all of the Grand Slam tournaments except the French Open.

Connors was the No. 1 player in the world for 160 weeks in a row, from July 29, 1974, to August 16, 1977. No man in the history of pro tennis has ever been No. 1 that many weeks in a row.

From 1973 through 1984, Connors was always one of the world's top three players. He was always in the top 10 until 1989. In fact, Connors won a record 109 singles titles from 1972 through 1989.

Connors's ranking dropped down to No. 936 in 1990 because he had to take time off for wrist surgery. But he surprised everyone in 1991 when he came back and reached the semifinals of the U.S. Open. He was thirty-nine years old, just like Rosewall was when Connors beat him in 1974.

"Looking back from the early 1990s, with Connors still playing well," Arthur Ashe said, "I see that he was the greatest male tennis player, bar none, in the two and a half decades since the Open era began in 1968."[4]

Jimmy Connors

BORN: September 2, 1952, Belleville, Illinois.

COLLEGE: UCLA.

PLAYS: Left-handed, two-handed backhand.

YEAR TURNED PRO: 1972.

GRAND SLAM TOURNAMENT SINGLES TITLES: (8); Australian Open
(1974), U.S. Open (1974, 1976, 1978, 1982–83), Wimbledon
(1974, 1982).

GRAND SLAM TOURNAMENT DOUBLES TITLES: (2); Wimbledon (1973);
U.S. Open (1975).

HONORS: Cofounder Champions Tour, 1993; U.S. Davis Cup team,
1976, 81, 84; International Tennis Federation World
Champion, 1982; NCAA champion, 1971.

Fierce determination shows on Jimmy Connors's face as he
takes a swat at the ball. When Connors retired, he ranked fifth
all-time in Grand Slam singles titles.

PANCHO GONZALES

Pancho Gonzales aims to put the ball out of reach. At twenty years old, Gonzales became the fifth youngest winner of the U.S. National Championship in 1948.

IT HAD BEEN A LONG MATCH. The first set lasted thirty-four games. Pancho Gonzales had lost the first two sets to Ted Schroeder, but came back to win the next two. "My only thought was to play as hard as I could," Gonzales said.[1]

Soon, Gonzales was one point from winning the 1949 U.S. National Championship, his second in a row.

No one had given Gonzales much credit for winning the U.S. National Championship at Forest Hills the previous year. At twenty, he was among the youngest champions the tournament ever had. But Schroeder had not played. Schroeder was thought to be the world's top amateur player.

So at match point in 1949, Gonzales raised his racquet to his lips and kissed it. He then banged his serve toward Schroeder. Schroeder ripped a forehand back to Gonzales. Gonzales got the ball back, but he hit it short. Schroeder moved in to smash the ball. Pow!

The ball sailed past Gonzales. It was out. Pancho Gonzales had done it! He had beaten Schroeder. Gonzales was the best in the world.

Gonzales had made a quick climb to the top. He had been twelve when he received his first tennis racquet. His mother had bought it for him for fifty cents.

By the time Gonzales was fifteen, he was the No. 1 player in southern California. He could not play in the national junior tournaments, however, because he was a Mexican American. "I felt like an outcast," Gonzales said.[2]

The Southern California Tennis Association eventually banned Gonzales from competition because he skipped school to play tennis. Gonzales later dropped out of school altogether in the tenth grade.

"All I want to do is to play tennis," Gonzales said. "From morning to night. My whole life long."[3]

Gonzales soon got his wish. After he won the U.S. national title in 1949, he turned pro. Gonzales struggled to beat Jack Kramer in his first year as a pro. But Gonzales was big (six feet three inches tall and 185 lbs.) and mean, and he had a very hard serve. He soon dominated the pro tour.

There were times when Gonzales didn't like professional tennis. It was too much business. "My idea of tennis was a fun sport," he said.[4] But Gonzales kept playing until he was in his mid-forties. By then, amateurs and pros were playing together in what is called open tennis.

"There were a lot of players who felt, 'Well, I can beat him,' because I was old," Gonzales said. "And there were a lot of players who were amazed that I could play as well as I did."[5]

In 1969, Gonzales, at forty-one, beat twenty-five-year-old Charlie Pasarell at Wimbledon in one of the greatest comebacks in tennis history. Gonzales finished the year ranked No. 6 in the world.

"Of all the players I have seen, I would have to rank Pancho No. 1," said Marty Riessen, a top 10 player in the 1970s. "At his best, he could beat everybody else."[6]

Pancho Gonzales

Born: May 9, 1928, Los Angeles, California.

Died: July 3, 1995.

Played: Right-handed, one-handed backhand.

Year Turned Pro: 1949.

Grand Slam Tournament Singles Titles: (2); U.S. Championships (1947–48).

Grand Slam Tournament Doubles Titles: (2); French Championships (1949); Wimbledon (1949).

Honors: Enshrined in International Tennis Hall of Fame, 1968; U.S. Davis Cup team, 1949.

Pancho Gonzales charges the net, and tries to put one past his opponent. Gonzales won a match at the Wimbledon tournament at the age of forty-one.

ROD LAVER

Rod Laver watches the ball skip across the court as he lines up his next shot in this picture from the 1969 U.S. Open. That year Laver defeated Tony Roche to win the title.

ROD LAVER

THE MOMENT ROD LAVER WON the Grand Slam in 1962, he was so stunned he could hardly think straight. "I don't remember going to the net to shake hands," said Laver, who turned pro in 1963.[1]

Then in 1969, Laver had the chance to win the Grand Slam again. It was amazing. No one before had ever had the chance to win two Grand Slams.

The rules did not allow pros to play in the Grand Slam tournaments (the Australian, French, British, and U.S. championships) until 1968. That is why Don Budge could not win another Grand Slam after he won history's first in 1938. Budge turned pro at the end of that year.

Laver, however, had the chance to become a living legend. Tennis was open to amateurs and pros.

One by one, Laver won the Australian Open, he won the French Open, and he won Wimbledon. Then in the U.S. Open on September 8, 1969, Laver punched a forehand volley cross court and watched as Tony Roche's return shot landed out. Laver won the tournament and his second Grand Slam.

United States Tennis Association President Alastair Martin told Laver he was perhaps the greatest tennis player ever. Laver said, "I never really think of myself in those terms, but I feel honored that people see fit to say such things about me."[2]

Laver was not a big man. He stood 5 feet 8 inches tall and weighed about 150 pounds. As a youngster growing up in Australia, he looked really small compared to other boys. But he was quick.

As soon as the famous Australian tennis coach Harry Hopman saw Laver, he called him "Rocket." Hopman also saw that Laver, at age sixteen, had great tennis skills.

"This kid's good all right," Hopman said. "Got all the shots."[3]

But Australia had many great tennis players. From 1950 through 1967, Australia won the Davis Cup all but three years. Players such as Lew Hoad and Ken Rosewall helped Australia dominate.

Laver was chosen for the Davis Cup team in 1957, but he did not play until 1959. He lost his first two Davis Cup matches. Laver also lost four of his first five major tournament finals.

But people still expected him to be great some day. "Give him a little more time. He'll be the best in the world," said Adrian Quist, the winningest player in Australian Davis Cup history.[4]

Laver won the Australian championship in 1960. He won Wimbledon in 1961. He won the Grand Slam in 1962.

Laver struggled his first couple of years as a pro in 1963 and 1964. But by 1966, he was beating all the pro players just like he used to beat all the amateurs.

Laver beat everyone, of course, once pros and amateurs started playing together in 1968. He was ranked No. 1 in the world in 1968 and 1969 and stayed in the top 10 until 1976.

"I remain unconvinced that there was ever a better player," said tennis commentator Bud Collins.[5]

ROD LAVER

BORN: August 9, 1938, Rockhampton, Queensland, Australia.

PLAYS: Left-handed, one-handed backhand.

YEAR TURNED PRO: 1963.

GRAND SLAM TOURNAMENT SINGLES TITLES: (11); Australian Open (1960, 1962, 1969), French Open (1962, 1969), U.S. Open (1962, 1969), Wimbledon (1961–62, 1968, 1969).

GRAND SLAM TOURNAMENT DOUBLES TITLES: (6); Australian Open (1959–61, 1969); French Championships (1961); Wimbledon (1971).

HONORS: Enshrined in International Tennis Hall of Fame, 1981; World Team Tennis Rookie of the Year, 1976; Australian Davis Cup team, 1959–62, 73; first player to reach $1 million in career earnings, 1971.

Rod Laver races across the court to get to the shot. Laver is the only man to win the Grand Slam twice.

JOHN MCENROE

JOHN MCENROE WAS NERVOUS. He was playing in his first Grand Slam tournament final. It was the 1979 U.S. Open in his hometown of New York. "I didn't think I got nervous in matches," McEnroe said.[1]

His nerves didn't really show in his play. McEnroe won the first two sets against his friend Vitas Gerulaitis and was three points from winning the third set and the match.

McEnroe punched a volley winner. He smacked a serve that Gerulaitis could not return. Then McEnroe smacked another winning serve. The match was over. Excited, McEnroe threw his racquet high into the air. He was the U.S. Open champion!

McEnroe, at age twenty, was the youngest U.S. national champ since Pancho Gonzales in 1948.

"When I was 18 and beat [Bjorn] Borg, they said I was the player of the future," McEnroe said. "Well, I think today I proved the future is now."[2]

McEnroe started playing tennis when he was eight years old. He only played then because his family had moved into a house near a tennis and swim club. Three years later, he started going to the Port Washington Tennis Academy. Harry Hopman, who coached Australian legends such as Rod Laver and Ken Rosewall, coached at Port Washington.

Soon, McEnroe was one of the best players. "I must admit I never thought John would become so good so quickly," said Tony Palafox, who helped coach McEnroe.[3]

The first time the world really heard about McEnroe was when he reached the semifinals at Wimbledon in 1977. His exceptional playing ability caught people's attention, but so

JOHN McENROE

John McEnroe grimaces as he slashes another backhand volley. McEnroe won the 1978 NCAA men's tennis championship during his time at Stanford University.

did his bad temper. The British newspapers nicknamed McEnroe "Super Brat."

McEnroe then became famous for his temper and arguing with the umpires—and fans. Arguing with the fans was the typical New Yorker thing to do, McEnroe explained. "When they started yelling at me, I would yell back at them," he said.[4]

Tennis officials fined McEnroe and suspended him many times during his career. The worst incident was at the Australian Open in 1990. McEnroe was kicked out of a match because he cursed officials.

Despite all of the arguing and shouting, McEnroe never seemed to lose his concentration. In fact, he often seemed to play better. And he was already one of the most talented tennis players the world had ever seen.

McEnroe won the U.S. Open three years in a row from 1979 to 1981 and won it again in 1984. He ended Bjorn Borg's five-year run as Wimbledon champion in 1981 and won the title himself three out of four years. McEnroe's Davis Cup record is the best in U.S. history. He won as many doubles titles (77) as he did singles titles.

McEnroe played tennis in a style no one had ever seen before. Even the former greats of the game were amazed. Arthur Ashe, who was McEnroe's Davis Cup captain, described McEnroe as "the kind of tennis player the world might see only once every 50 years."[5]

JOHN McENROE

BORN: February 16, 1959, Wiesbaden, Germany.

COLLEGE: Stanford University.

PLAYS: Left-handed, one-handed backhand.

YEAR TURNED PRO: 1978.

GRAND SLAM TOURNAMENT SINGLES TITLES: (7); U.S. Open (1979–81, 1984), Wimbledon (1981, 1983–84).

GRAND SLAM TOURNAMENT DOUBLES TITLES: (9); Wimbledon (1979, 1981, 1983–84, 1992); U.S. Open (1979, 1981, 1983, 1989).

HONORS: U.S. Davis Cup team, 1978–84, 1987–89, 1991–92; No. 1 in U.S. Davis Cup total victories (59); No. 1 in U.S. Davis Cup singles victories (41); NCAA champion, 1978.

Many feel that McEnroe's personality made him one of the most entertaining players of all-time.

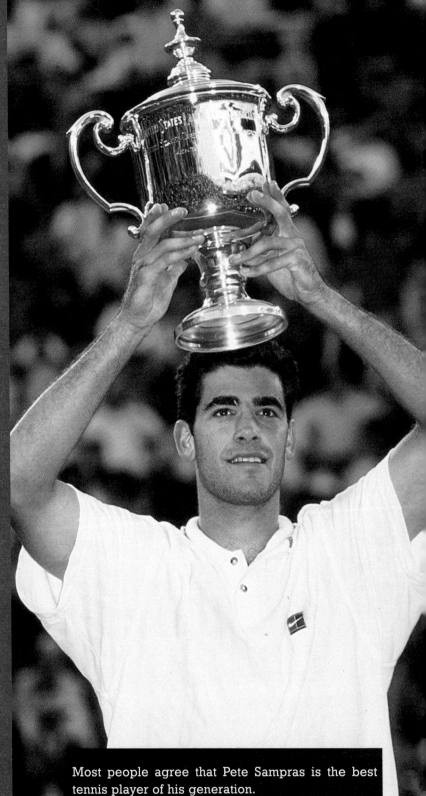

PETE SAMPRAS

Most people agree that Pete Sampras is the best tennis player of his generation.

PETE SAMPRAS

PETE SAMPRAS WAS AT THE TOP of the list of people who didn't think he could win the 1990 U.S. Open. "Maybe in a couple of years," he said, after winning his third match in the tournament, "but I don't think it's realistic right now. I'm just going out there and trying to win every match and see what happens. But it's very tough for the way I play at age 19 to win a Grand Slam."[1]

Sampras was right. More experienced players usually win the Grand Slam tournaments (the Australian Open, the French Open, Wimbledon, and the U.S. Open). But Sampras had a great serve. He hit the ball as fast as 120 mph. He used his powerful serve to beat two players who used to be ranked No. 1 in the world, Ivan Lendl and John McEnroe.

After he beat McEnroe, Sampras, who was ranked No. 12, played No. 4 Andre Agassi for the U.S. Open championship. On the second point of the match, Sampras hit a serve so fast Agassi couldn't touch it. Ace! Sampras aced Agassi 13 times that afternoon.

Agassi and Sampras had been playing for one hour and forty-two minutes when Agassi served the last ball of the match. Sampras hit it back, deep in the court. Agassi hit his next shot into the net. Sampras won the match and the U.S. Open championship.

At age nineteen, Sampras was the youngest man ever to win the tournament. "It was the best I could possibly play," he said. "I really don't know if anyone could have beaten me."[2]

Few people thought Sampras would be successful when he dropped out of high school in Rancho Palos Verdes,

California, and turned pro at age sixteen. He had not won any major junior tournaments, and his ranking had fallen when he changed from a two-handed backhand to a one-handed backhand.

"I remember one pro saying that another ranked junior was going to be a better player; another pro saying Pete wouldn't make it at all," said Dr. Pete Fischer, Sampras's coach from age seven to eighteen.[3]

But Fischer knew better. He had instructed Sampras to study videotapes of former tennis champions such as Rod Laver and Ken Rosewall. Sampras learned to act like a champion and to play like a champion.

It took another two and a half years after winning the 1990 U.S. Open for Sampras to become No. 1 in the world. By then, he had another coach, Tim Gullikson. Gullikson taught Sampras how to be mentally tough and to always play hard, no matter what.

That new attitude made Sampras an even better player. He won three Grand Slam tournaments in a row: Wimbledon and the U.S. Open in 1993 and the Australian Open in 1994.

Winning Wimbledon was particularly special for Sampras. "You can come over to London as No. 1 in the world," Sampras said, "but nobody thinks you're anybody until you've won Wimbledon."[4]

Sampras won the tournament three years in a row. No other American had ever done that. Pete Sampras was definitely somebody.

PETE SAMPRAS

BORN: August 12, 1971, Washington, D.C.

PLAYS: Right-handed, one-handed backhand.

YEAR TURNED PRO: 1988.

GRAND SLAM TOURNAMENT SINGLES TITLES: (10); Australian Open
(1994, 1997); U.S. Open (1990, 1993, 1995–96); Wimbledon
(1993–95, 1997).

HONORS: U.S. Davis Cup team, 1991–92, 1994–95; International
Tennis Federation World Champion, 1993–95; ATP Tour
Player of the Year, 1993–94; Jim Thorpe Tennis Player of
the Year, 1993.

As he awaits the serve, Sampras gets set to spring into action.

BILL TILDEN

NO ONE KNEW IT, BUT Bill Tilden was in complete control when he lost the first set of the 1920 Wimbledon men's singles final. He didn't worry at all when Gerald Patterson won the set 6-2.

Tilden looked at the people sitting around the court. He saw a friend and grinned. "Immediately, Bill proceeded to play," said the friend, actress Peggy Wood.[1]

Tilden pounded Patterson in the next three sets 6-3, 6-2, 6-4. Tilden became the first American man to win Wimbledon. He shook Patterson's hand and ran off the court. "I'm too happy to speak," he said.[2]

From 1920 to 1926, Tilden won almost every tournament he played. He was so good, he would sometimes start losing a match on purpose and then come back to win.

People called Tilden "Big Bill." He was six feet one inch tall, which was taller than many tennis players. He also had a powerful cannonball serve.

Tilden learned to play tennis at his family's summer home in the Catskill Mountains of New York when he was five years old. But it took many years for him to become a great player. When he first went to college at the University of Pennsylvania, he wasn't good enough to make the varsity tennis team.

"From the age of 12 to about 19 or 20," Tilden said, "I played pretty badly."[3]

But Tilden was willing to practice and work hard to get better. Early in his career, he didn't have a good backhand. Bill Johnston beat Tilden in the 1919 U.S. National Championships because of that. So Tilden moved to

BILL TILDEN

Tennis has changed a great deal since Bill Tilden's time. Notice the difference between what he is wearing and what the players wear today.

Providence, Rhode Island, for the winter and practiced his backhand every day.

After that, Tilden became unbeatable. He won Wimbledon in 1920 and 1921. He won the U.S. National Championships every year from 1920 to 1925. He won 16 consecutive Davis Cup singles matches.

Even after Frenchman Henri Cochet beat Tilden at the 1926 U.S. National Championships, Tilden came back and won the tournament for the seventh time in 1929. The next year, Tilden won his third Wimbledon title. He was thirty-seven years old.

The 1920s were called the Golden Age of Sports because so many of the greatest athletes of all time were at their best then. There was Babe Ruth in baseball. There was Red Grange in football. There was Jack Dempsey in boxing. And there was "Big Bill" Tilden in tennis.

In 1969, tennis players from all over the world named Tilden the greatest tennis player of all time.

"He had the equipment to beat them all—past and present," said Frank Hunter, Tilden's doubles partner and Davis Cup teammate. "There's never been anyone like him."[4]

BILL TILDEN

BORN: February 10, 1893, Philadelphia, Pennsylvania.

DIED: June 5, 1953.

COLLEGE: University of Pennsylvania.

PLAYED: Right-handed, one-handed backhand.

YEAR TURNED PRO: 1931.

GRAND SLAM TOURNAMENT SINGLES TITLES: (10); U.S. Championships (1920–25, 1929), Wimbledon (1920–21, 1930).

GRAND SLAM TOURNAMENT DOUBLES TITLES: (6); Wimbledon (1927); U.S. Championships (1918, 1921–23, 1927).

HONORS: Enshrined in International Tennis Hall of Fame, 1959; U.S. Davis Cup team, 1920–30; U.S. Davis Cup captain, 1928; German Davis Cup captain, 1937.

Known as "Big Bill," Tilden dominated the sport of tennis in the 1920s. Tilden was the No. 1 ranked player, 1920–25.

CHAPTER NOTES

Andre Agassi
1. Robin Finn, "Agassi's Ascendance Righted All the Wrongs," *The New York Times*, September 13, 1994, p. B12.
2. Sally Jenkins, "Love and Love," *Sports Illustrated*, March 13, 1995, p. 57.
3. Olympic Games press conference (August 3, 1996).

Arthur Ashe
1. Will Grimsley, *Tennis: Its History, People, and Events* (Englewood Cliffs, N.J.: Prentice-Hall, 1971), p. 124.
2. Arthur Ashe with Frank Deford, *Arthur Ashe: Portrait in Motion* (New York: Houghton Mifflin, 1975), p. 273.
3. Kenny Moore, "He Did All He Could," *Sports Illustrated*, February 15, 1993, p. 15.

Bjorn Borg
1. David Irvine, "Wimbledon '80: Borg's & McEnroe's Rendezvous With Tennis History," *Tennis*, September 1980, p. 102.
2. Bjorn Borg and Eugene L. Scott, *Bjorn Borg: My Life and Game* (New York: Simon and Schuster, 1980), p. 75.
3. Ibid., p. 14.
4. Ibid., p. 61.
5. Jennifer Frey, "For Borg, Tennis Again a Love Game," *The Washington Post*, May 10, 1996, p. C3.

Don Budge
1. Don Budge, "The Man Who Invented the Grand Slam," *The Tennis Book* ed. Michael Bartlett and Bob Gillen (New York: Arbor House Publishing Company, 1981), p. 184.
2. Ibid., p. 176.
3. Stan Hart, *Once a Champion* (New York: Dodd, Mead & Company, 1985), p. 148.
4. Allison Danzig, "The Story of J. Donald Budge," *Budge on Tennis* ed. J. Donald Budge (New York: Prentice-Hall, Inc., 1939), p. 29.

Jimmy Connors
1. Joe Jares, "For Love and Money," *Sports Illustrated*, July 15, 1974, p. 19.
2. Susie Trees, "Here's to the Winners," *World Tennis*, April 1978, p. 46.
3. Richard Evans, *Open Tennis: 1968–1988* (Lexingon, Mass.: The Stephen Greene Press, 1989), p. 129.
4. Arthur Ashe and Arnold Rampersad, *Days of Grace* (New York: Alfred A. Knopf, 1993), p. 75.

Pancho Gonzales
1. Will Grimsley, *Tennis: Its History, People, and Events* (Englewood Cliffs, N.J.: Prentice-Hall, Inc., 1971), p. 95.
2. Andrea Leand, "The Lone Wolf," *Tennis Week*, July 20, 1995, p. 19.
3. Gianni Clerici, "Pancho Gonzales" *Tales From the Tennis Court* ed. Richard Evans (London: Sidgwick & Jackson, 1983), p. 164.

4. Leand, p. 19.

5. Personal interview with Pancho Gonzales (August 24, 1993).

6. Marty Riessen and Richard Evans, *Match Point: A Candid View of Life on the International Tennis Circuit* (Englewood Cliffs, N.J.: Prentice-Hall, 1973), p. 113.

Rod Laver

1. Will Grimsley, *Tennis: Its History, People, and Events* (Englewood Cliffs, N.J.: Prentice-Hall, Inc., 1971), p. 116.

2. Bud Collins and Zander Hollander, *Bud Collins' Modern Encyclopedia of Tennis*, 2nd ed. (Detroit: Visible Ink Press, 1994), p. 171.

3. Grimsley, p. 112.

4. Dave Anderson, "The Rocket," *The Fireside Book of Tennis* ed. Allison Danzig and Peter Schwed (New York: Simon and Schuster, 1972), p. 411.

5. Bud Collins, *My Life with the Pros* (New York: E. P. Dutton, 1989), p. 268.

John McEnroe

1. Danny Robbins, "Austin dethrones Lloyd," *Philadelphia Inquirer*, September 10, 1979, p. 6-C.

2. Ray Didinger, "McEnroe Captures an Unstuffy Open," *Philadelphia Bulletin*, September 10, 1979, p. 30.

3. Richard Evans, *McEnroe: A Rage for Perfection* (New York: Simon and Schuster, 1982), pp. 34–35.

4. Samantha Stevenson, "McEnroe and Connors Agree: There Is No One Around Quite Like Them," *The New York Times*, August 4, 1996, Sports Sunday, p. 9.

5. Arthur Ashe and Arnold Rampersad, *Days of Grace* (New York: Alfred A. Knopf, 1993), p. 69.

Pete Sampras

1. Eliot Berry, *Tough Draw: The Path to Tennis Glory* (New York: Henry Holt and Company, 1992), p. 194.

2. Sally Jenkins, "With an Ace Up His Sleeve, Sampras Played Cards Right," *The Washington Post*, September 11, 1990, p. E1.

3. David Higdon, "Pete Sampras: Dreams Do Come True," *Tennis*, January 1991, p. 35.

4. Robin Finn, "Making Mr. Wimbledon: Gullikson Taught Sampras to Embrace Grass," *The New York Times*, June 23, 1996, Sports Sunday, p. 5.

Bill Tilden

1. Frank Deford, "Big Bill Tilden," *Tales From the Tennis Court* ed. Richard Evans (London: Sidgwick & Jackson, 1983), p. 61.

2. Capt. B. H. Liddell-Hart, "English Championship Story Continued," *American Lawn Tennis*, August 1, 1920, p. 301.

3. Alan J. Gould, "Tilden Spells It Out," *The Fireside Book of Tennis* ed. Allison Danzig and Peter Schwed (New York: Simon and Schuster, 1972), p. 169.

4. Allison Danzig, "The Greatest of All Time," *The Fireside Book of Tennis*, p. 177.

Index

A
Agassi, Andre, 4, 6–9, 39
Agassi, Mike, 7
Ashe, Arthur, 10–13, 24, 36
Ashe, Jeanne Moutoussamy, 12

B
Bergelin, Lennart, 15
Bollettieri, Nick, 8
Borg, Bjorn, 7, 14–17, 34, 36
Budge, Don, 4, 18–21, 31
Budge, Lloyd, 18

C
Charity, Ronald, 10
Cochet, Henri, 44
Collins, Bud, 32
Connors, Gloria, 22
Connors, Jimmy, 12, 22–25

D
Dempsey, Jack, 44

F
Fischer, Dr. Pete, 40
Frazier, Joe, 22

G
Gerulaitis, Vitas, 34
Gilbert, Brad, 8
Gonzales, Pancho, 5, 26–29, 34
Grange, Red, 44
Gullikson, Tim, 40

H
Hitler, Adolf, 20
Hoad, Lew, 4, 32
Hopman, Harry 32, 34
Hunter, Frank, 44

J
Johnson, Dr. Robert Walter, 10
Johnston, Bill, 42

K
Kramer, Jack, 10, 28

L
Laver, Rod, 5, 30–33, 34, 40
Lendl, Ivan, 4, 39

M
Mako, Gene, 18
Martin, Alastair, 31
McEnroe, John, 15, 34–37, 39

N
Nastase, Ilie, 7, 16

O
Okker, Tom, 10

P
Palafox, Tony, 34
Parun, Onny, 16
Pasarell, Charlie, 28
Pate, Walter, 20
Patterson, Gerald, 42
Perry, Fred, 20

Q
Quist, Adrian, 32

R
Riessen, Marty, 28
Riggs, Bobby, 7
Roche, Tony, 31
Rosewall, Ken, 4, 22, 24, 32, 34, 40
Ruth, Babe, 44

S
Sampras, Pete, 4, 7, 38–41
Schroeder, Ted, 27
Stich, Michael, 7
Stockton, Dick, 22

T
Tilden, Bill, 4, 42–45

V
von Cramm, Baron Gottfried, 20

W
Wood, Peggy, 42